Montville Township Public Library
90  Horseneck Road
Montville,  N.J.  07045-9626
973-402-0900

Library Hours

| | |
|---|---|
| Monday | 9 a.m.-9 p.m. |
| Tuesday | 9 a.m.-9 p.m. |
| Wednesday | 9 a.m.-9 p.m. |
| Thursday | 9 a.m.-9 p.m. |
| Friday | 9 a.m.-6 p.m. |
| Saturday | 9 a.m.-5 p.m. |
| Sunday | 12 p.m.-5 p.m. |

see website  www.montvillelibrary.org

# AMAZING ORiGAMi

# Origami Sea Creatures

Lisa Miles

Gareth Stevens
Publishing

**Please visit our website, www.garethstevens.com. For a free color catalog of all our high-quality books, call toll free 1-800-542-2595 or fax 1-877-542-2596.**

Library of Congress Cataloging-in-Publication Data

Miles, Lisa.
 Origami sea creatures / Lisa Miles.
    pages cm. —  (Amazing origami)
 Includes index.
ISBN 978-1-4339-9661-0 (pbk.)
ISBN 978-1-4339-9662-7 (6-pack)
 ISBN 978-1-4339-9660-3 (library binding)
1.  Origami—Juvenile literature. 2.  Marine animals—Juvenile literature.  I. Title.
 TT872.5.M558 2013
 736'.982—dc23
                                        2012050331

First Edition

Published in 2014 by
**Gareth Stevens Publishing**
111 East 14th Street, Suite 349
New York, NY 10003

Copyright © 2014 Arcturus Publishing

Models and photography: Belinda Webster and Michael Wiles
Text: Lisa Miles
Design: Emma Randall
Editors: Anna Brett, Becca Clunes, and Joe Harris
Animal photography: Shutterstock

Printed in the United States of America

CPSIA compliance information: Batch #CS13GS: For further information contact Gareth Stevens, New York, New York at 1-800-542-2595.

# Contents

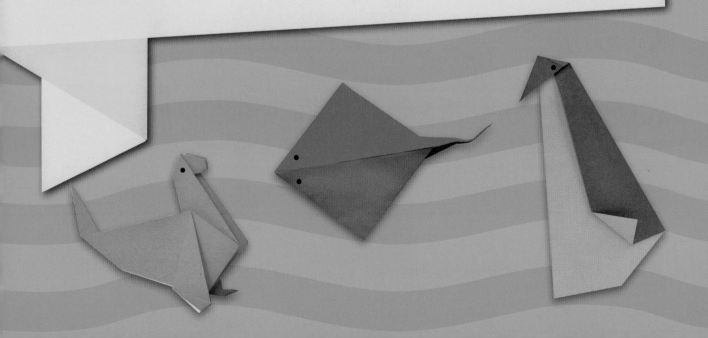

# Basic Folds

**Origami has been popular in Japan for hundreds of years and is now loved all around the world. You can make great origami models with just one sheet of paper... and this book shows you how!**

The paper used in origami is thin but strong, so that it can be folded many times. It is usually colored on one side. You can also use ordinary scrap paper, but make sure it's not too thick.

Origami models often share the same folds and basic designs, known as "bases." This introduction explains some of the folds and bases that you will need for the projects in this book. When making the models, follow the key below to find out what the lines and arrows mean. And always crease well!

## KEY

valley fold ------------

mountain fold ················

step fold (mountain and valley fold next to each other)

direction to move paper

push ◀

## MOUNTAIN FOLD

*To make a mountain fold, fold the paper so that the crease is pointing up toward you, like a mountain.*

## VALLEY FOLD

*To make a valley fold, fold the paper the other way, so that the crease is pointing away from you, like a valley.*

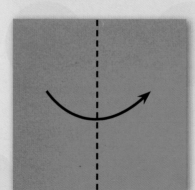

# INSIDE REVERSE FOLD

An inside reverse fold is useful if you want to make a nose or a tail, or if you want to flatten the shape of another part of an origami model.

**1** Practice by first folding a piece of paper diagonally in half. Make a valley fold on one point and crease.

**2** It's important to make sure that the paper is creased well. Run your finger over the crease two or three times.

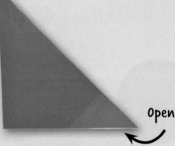

Open

**3** Unfold and open up the corner slightly. Refold the crease nearest to you into a mountain fold.

**4** Open up the paper a little more and then tuck the tip of the point inside. Close the paper. This is the view from the underside of the paper.

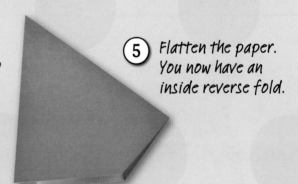

**5** Flatten the paper. You now have an inside reverse fold.

# OUTSIDE REVERSE FOLD

An outside reverse fold is useful if you want to make a head, beak, foot, or another part of your model that sticks out.

**1** Practice by first folding a piece of paper diagonally in half. Make a valley fold on one point and crease.

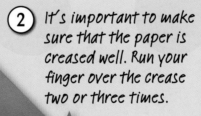

**2** It's important to make sure that the paper is creased well. Run your finger over the crease two or three times.

**3** Unfold and open up the corner slightly. Refold the crease farthest away from you into a valley fold.

Open

**4** Open up the paper a little more and start to turn the corner inside out. Then close the paper when the fold begins to turn.

**5** You now have an outside reverse fold. You can either flatten the paper or leave it rounded out.

# Bases

## WATERBOMB BASE

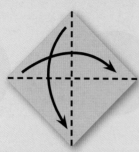

**1** Start with a square of paper, the point turned toward you. Make two diagonal valley folds.

**2** The paper should now look like this. Turn it over.

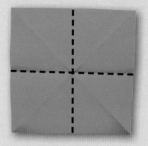

**3** Make two valley folds along the horizontal and vertical lines.

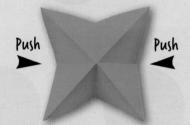

Push          Push

**4** Push the paper into this shape, so the center spot pops up.

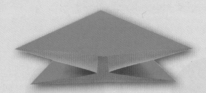

**5** Push the sides in, bringing the back and front sections together.

**6** Flatten the paper. You now have a waterbomb base.

## KITE BASE

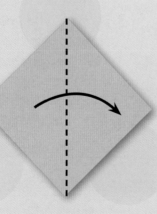

**1** Start with the point turned toward you. Valley fold it in half diagonally.

**2** Valley fold the left section to meet the center crease.

**3** Do the same on the other side.

**4** You now have a kite base.

# BIRD BASE

**(1)** Follow the first four steps of the Waterbomb base. The paper should look like this.

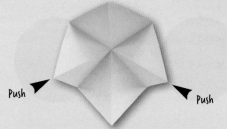

**(2)** Hold the paper by opposite diagonal corners. Push the two corners together so that the shape begins to collapse. It should collapse into a square.

**(3)** Turn the open end to face you. Then valley fold the top left flap to the center crease.

**(4)** Do the same on the other side.

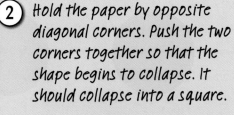

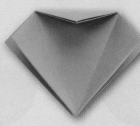

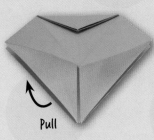

**(5)** Valley fold the top triangle.

**(6)** Unfold the top and sides and you have the shape shown here.

**(7)** Take the bottom corner and begin to open out the upper flap by gently pulling upwards.

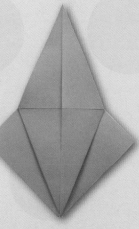

**(8)** The paper should open like a bird's beak. Open out the flap as far as it will go.

**(9)** Flatten the paper so that you now have this shape. Turn the paper over.

**(10)** The paper should now look like this. Repeat steps 3 through 9 on this side.

**(11)** You now have a bird base. The two flaps at the bottom are separated by an open slit.

# Penguin

The penguin is a great swimmer, but it waddles on land. So don't worry if your origami model wobbles—it just makes it more realistic!

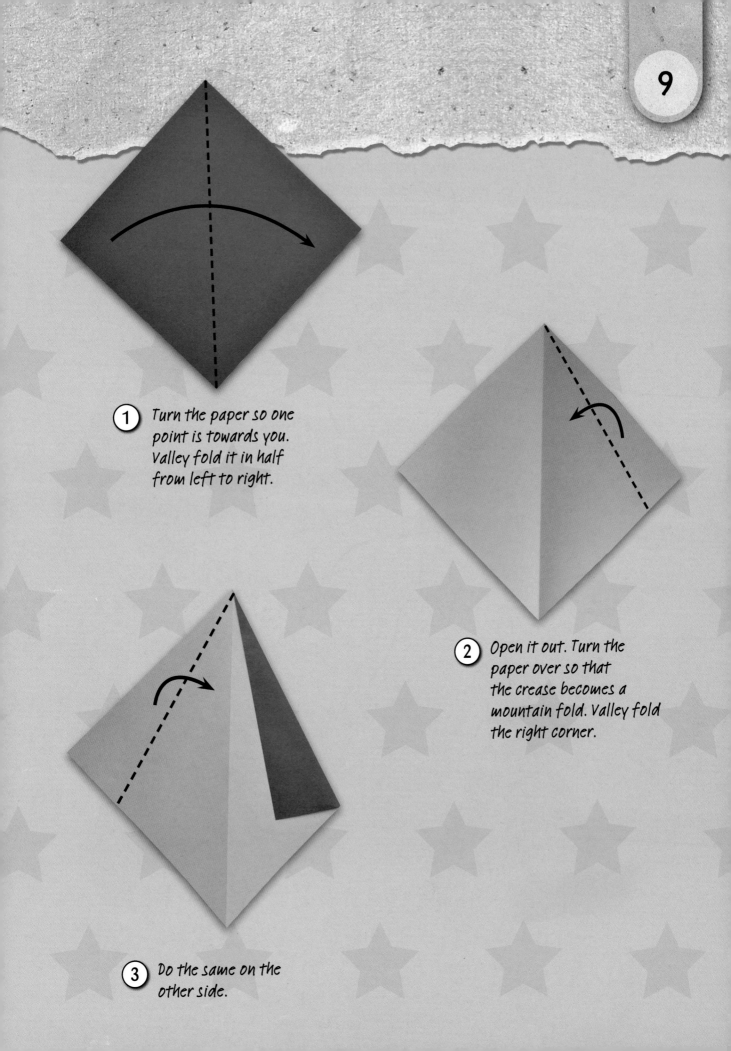

1. Turn the paper so one point is towards you. Valley fold it in half from left to right.

2. Open it out. Turn the paper over so that the crease becomes a mountain fold. Valley fold the right corner.

3. Do the same on the other side.

## Did You Know?

When you think of penguins, you probably think of ice and snow. However, some species of penguins live in tropical climates!

④ The paper should now look like this.

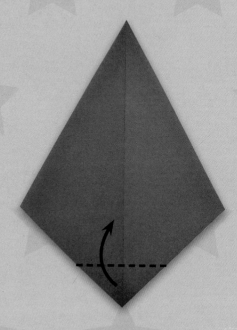

⑤ Turn the paper over and valley fold the bottom.

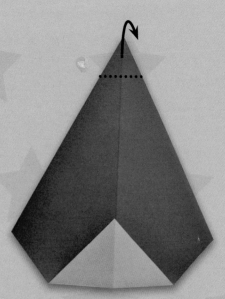

⑥ Mountain fold the top of the paper over.

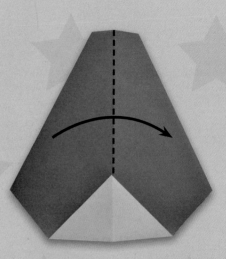

⑦ Valley fold the paper in half from left to right.

Pull

(8) Valley fold the corner tip. This is the penguin's wing. Do the same on the other side.

(9) Now pull up the beak.

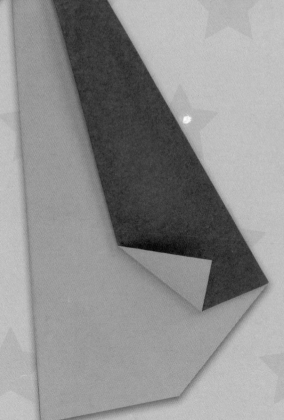

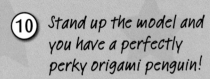

(10) Stand up the model and you have a perfectly perky origami penguin!

# Whale

The blue whale is the largest animal to have ever existed. It can measure up to 98 feet (30 m) long—that's about 200 times longer than your origami model!

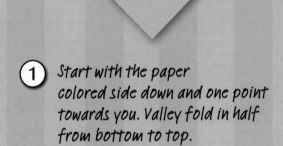

1. Start with the paper colored side down and one point towards you. Valley fold in half from bottom to top.

2. Open the paper out. Turn it over, so that the center crease is now a mountain fold. Fold down the top corner diagonally the other way.

3. Do the same on the other side.

## Did You Know?

Blue whales sing to each other under water. They can hear each other's calls over distances of 100 miles (160 km) away!

**4** Fold back the tip of the top corner.

**5** Do the same on the other side.

**6** Mountain fold the left side of the paper.

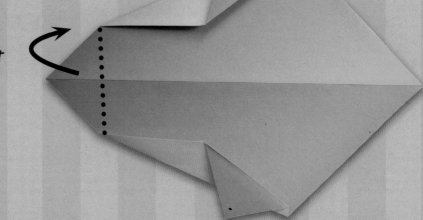

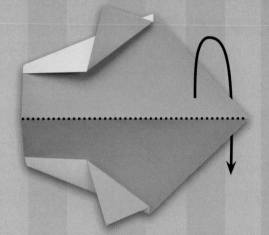

**7** Mountain fold the paper in half along the center crease, so that the top folds under the bottom.

**8** Mountain fold the right corner. Unfold, then make an inside reverse fold to create the tail.

**9** Now draw a smiley face—and you have an origami whale!

# Seal

The seal is clumsy on land and uses its flippers to pull itself along. In the sea, though, it speeds through the water, twisting and turning.

Start with a kite base

**1** Make a kite base, as shown on page 6. Valley fold the left corner.

**2** Do the same on the other side.

**3** The paper should look like this.

open

**4** Open out the top left corner. Take hold of the inside flap and pull it down to meet the center crease to make a new flap, as shown.

open

**5** Flatten the paper. Then do the same on the other side.

**6** The paper should now look like this.

# Did You Know?

Seals are mammals and breathe air. However, they can hold their breath underwater for nearly 2 hours!

**7** With the flaps pointing right, fold it in half so that the bottom goes under the top section.

**8** Mountain fold the left point.

**9** Unfold, then make an inside reverse fold to create the seal's neck.

**10** Looking from above, you should now be able to see the inside reverse fold, as shown above.

**11** Mountain fold the top point.

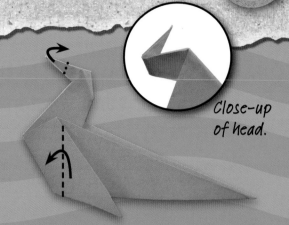

Close-up
of head.

12 Unfold, then make an inside reverse fold to create the seal's head.

13 Valley fold the flippers forward on both sides. Mountain fold the tip of the seal's head.

14 Unfold, then tuck in the seal's nose to make it blunt. Mountain fold the right point.

15 Unfold, then make an inside reverse fold to create the tail. On one of the flippers, valley fold the tip of the flap.

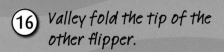

16 Valley fold the tip of the other flipper.

17 Now your origami seal is standing up and ready to clap its flippers!

# Dolphin

Medium

Dolphins are supposed to bring good luck to sailors.
Maybe this origami version will do the same for you!

**Start with a waterbomb base**

1. Find out how to make a waterbomb base on page 6. Valley fold the upper flap on the left.

2. Valley fold the top right section, as shown.

3. Valley fold the top right flap. This will make the fin on the dolphin's back.

## Did You Know?

Killer whales are not really whales at all.
They're actually a kind of large dolphin.

**4** Valley fold the left side of the paper across the other folds to make a sharp point. This is the nose.

**5** Step fold the nose by doing a valley fold and then a mountain fold. This makes it extra pointy!

**6** Mountain fold the right corner so that it points straight down. This is the tail.

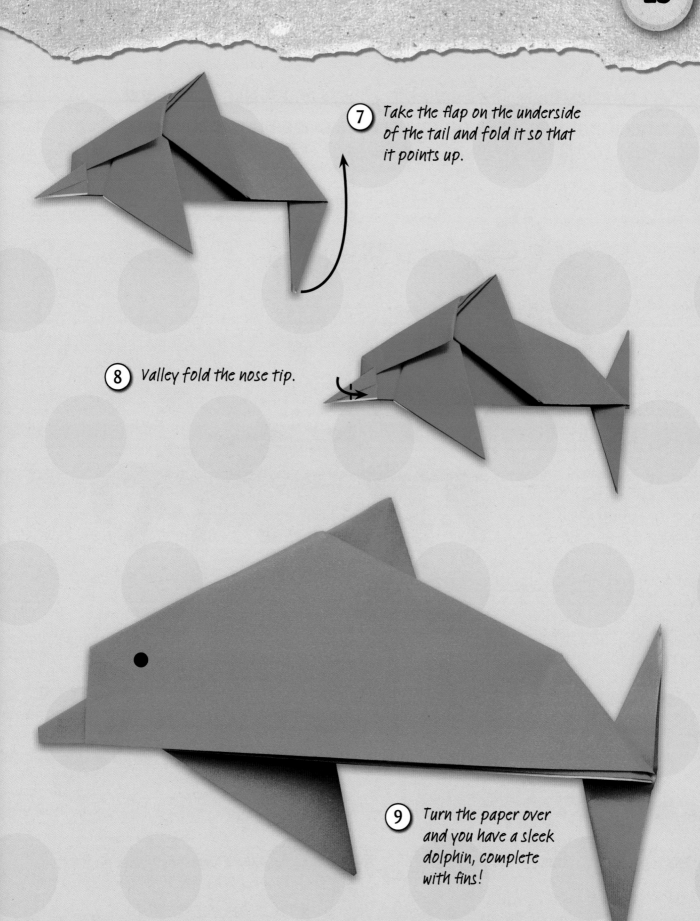

7 Take the flap on the underside of the tail and fold it so that it points up.

8 Valley fold the nose tip.

9 Turn the paper over and you have a sleek dolphin, complete with fins!

# Crab

A crab has eight legs, two big claws, and walks sideways!
Check out the claws on this simple origami model.

**Start with a waterbomb base**

1 Find out how to make a waterbomb base on page 6. Mountain fold the upper flap on the right, so that it tucks behind itself.

## Did You Know?

Fiddler crabs are strange looking creatures. They have one large claw and one little one.

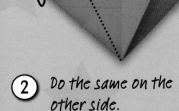

**2** Do the same on the other side.

**3** You should now have this shape. Make sure the two points at the top line up in the center.

**4** Turn the paper over. Valley fold the bottom corner.

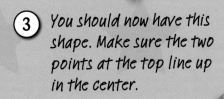

**5** Valley fold the right corner.

**6** Do the same on the other side.

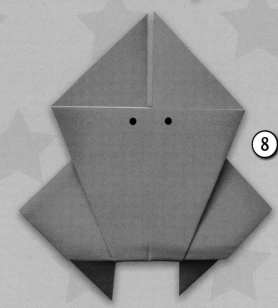

**8** Turn the paper over... and you will have an origami crab!

**7** You should now have a simplified crab shape.

# Shark

Sharks glide through the water in search of prey. This dangerous-looking origami shark has its mouth open wide, ready to bite.

**Start with a bird base**

① Find out how to make a bird base on page 7. The open slit points down. Take the upper, top flap and step fold it as shown.

② Take the right flap on the top layer and valley fold it along the center crease.

## Did You Know?

Sharks have many teeth arranged in rows. When they lose teeth from the front row, new ones move forward to fill the gap.

**3** Take the bottom point and valley fold it up along the center crease, then mountain fold down to make another step fold.

**4** Take the flap on the bottom layer of the left side and swing it back under the right side. Flatten it.

Pull

**5** You should now have two points at the top and one point at the bottom. Take the top left point and pull it down into the position shown in step 6.

**6** Flatten the paper. Valley fold it in half along the center crease, from right to left.

**7** Turn it on its side, as shown. The shark's nose is on the left and its tail is on the right. Mountain fold the right point.

**8** You have the beginnings of the tail as above. Unfold and make an outside reverse fold to finish the tail.

**9** Now you have a sharp-looking origami shark with a wide-open mouth!

# Ray

The ray has a flat body so that it can glide easily through the water. Watch out—some rays can give you a nasty electric shock!

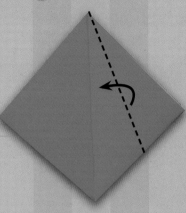

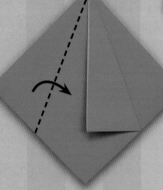

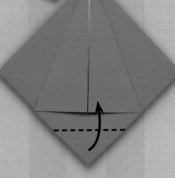

(1) Follow the first two steps of the bird base on page 7. Then turn your square so that the open ends are at the top, and fold in the upper flap on the top right.

(2) Do the same on the other side.

(3) Valley fold the bottom triangle up.

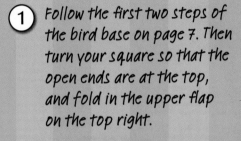

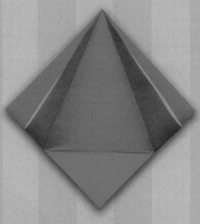

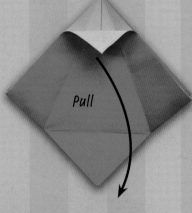

Pull

(4) Open out the folds that you made in steps 1–3.

(5) The paper should now look like this, opened out.

(6) Gently pull the upper flap out towards you to open up the center of the paper.

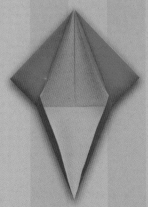

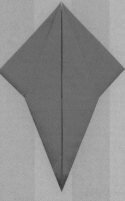

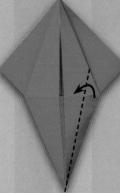

(7) Pull it out until it looks like an open bird's beak.

(8) Now flatten the paper so that it looks like this.

(9) Valley fold the right side of the paper to meet the center crease.

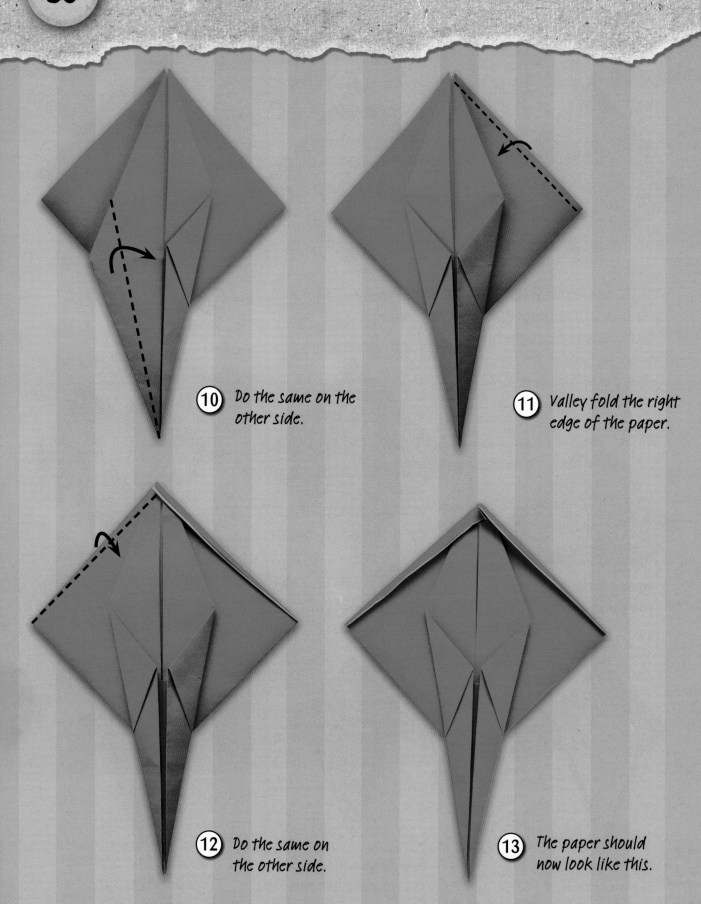

10 Do the same on the other side.

11 Valley fold the right edge of the paper.

12 Do the same on the other side.

13 The paper should now look like this.

# Did You Know?

Electric rays can stun their prey with an electric shock.

(14) Turn the paper over. Mountain fold carefully along the body and tail.

(15) Bend and pinch the tail to give it shape. Shape it how you like!

(16) Unfold and now you have an origami ray with a zigzagging tail!

# Glossary

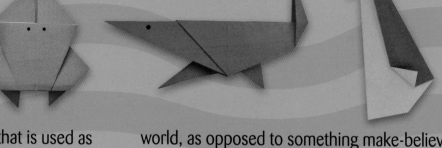

**base** A simple, folded shape that is used as the starting point for many different origami projects.

**crease** A line in a piece of paper made by folding.

**flipper** A flat limb used by a sea creature to push itself through water.

**mammal** A warm-blooded animal that gives birth to live young.

**mountain fold** An origami step where a piece of paper is folded so that the crease is pointing upwards, like a mountain.

**realistic** Looking like something from the real world, as opposed to something make-believe.

**step fold** A mountain fold and valley fold next to each other.

**tropical** From a hot part of the world.

**valley fold** An origami step where a piece of paper is folded so that the crease is pointing downwards, like a valley.

**waddle** To walk with short steps, swaying from side to side.

**waterbomb** A traditional origami shape, which can be filled with water.

# Further Reading

Robinson, Nick. *Absolute Beginner's Origami.* New York: Potter Craft, 2006.

Robinson, Nick. *World's Best Origami.* New York: Alpha Books, 2010.

Van Sicklen, Margaret. *Origami on the Go: 40 Paper-Folding Projects for Kids Who Love to Travel.* New York: Workman Publishing Company, 2009.

# Index